ıt

Christian Churches

Marcus Ward

Ward Lock Educational

ISBN 0 7062 3597 5
First published 1970
Reprinted January 1973
Reprinted November 1973

© Ward Lock Educational 1970. All rights reserved. No part of this publication may be reproduced stored in a retrieval system, or transmitted, in any form or by any means, electronic, mechanical, photocopying, recording or otherwise, without the prior permission of the copyright owner.

Reprinted 1976

Set in 11 on 12 point Press Roman on an IBM 72 Composer
for Ward Lock Educational Company Limited
116 Baker Street, London W1M 2BB

Printed in Spain by Editorial fher s.a.

Contents

Acknowledgments   4

1 What Christians believe   5

2 The Protestant Reformation   14

3 The Church of England   20

4 The Presbyterian Churches   30

5 The Separatist Protestant Churches   35

6 Methodism   40

7 In faith to unity   44

Suggestions for further reading   46

Index   47

Acknowledgments

The author and publishers wish to thank the following for their help in providing the photographs and drawings which illustrate this book: Barnaby's Picture Library pp 8, 43; Elizabeth Clarke pp 16, 22, 26, 31, 42; W.R. Hawes pp 10, 11 top, 20; Keystone Press pp 11 bottom, 13; Presbyterian Historical Society p 33; SPCK p 29.

1   What Christians believe

All Christians, no matter which part of the Church they belong to, have
certain major beliefs in common – they believe in one God and accept the
authority of His word revealed in the Bible and try to follow the teaching
of Jesus Christ. Where Protestants differ from Roman Catholics will be
shown later.

God: the Holy Trinity
Christians believe that there is one God, the maker and ruler of all things. He
is all-powerful, all-knowing, all-loving and present everywhere. He will bring to
pass his holy and loving purposes. The one God has made himself known to
men as Father, and as Son, and as Holy Spirit (Ghost). This is the meaning of
the Holy Trinity – one God in all three persons. God, the loving Father of mankind, so loved the world that he sent his only Son, Jesus Christ, to save all
men from sin. The Son of God came down to live on earth as Jesus. He took
all the sins of mankind upon himself and died so that these sins could be
forgiven. The Holy Spirit is the spirit of God who can enter into man and bring
him close to the Father. Jesus before he died promised his disciples that when
he left them the Holy Spirit would come upon them and give them the strength
they would need to be witnesses to him. So Christians believe concerning the
Holy Trinity that God the Father, God the Son and God the Holy Spirit are
one God, each of them active in the salvation of mankind.

The Holy Bible
Christians believe that the will and purpose of God has been revealed to man
through the Bible which is therefore for them the main source of truth and
conduct. Most Protestants would say the only source. All that is necessary
for salvation can be found in the Bible and Christians regard it as the ultimate
authority on all matters of truth.
   The Bible is divided into two main parts – the Old and the New
Testaments. The Old Testament is a series of books telling the history of the
Jews as the people of God, to whom He first revealed Himself. Throughout
the Old Testament the prophets had spoken of a Messiah (an anointed one)
who would come to prepare the way on earth for the kingdom of God. The
New Testament is an account, as told by his followers, of the life of the man
whom Christians believe fulfilled the prophecy, Jesus the Messiah, i.e. Christ,
and of the beginnings of the Church which founded the new people of God.

5

Jesus of Nazareth

God sent His only son, Jesus Christ, to show men the way to salvation. His perfect example showed them what it is to be a man as God intended man to be. It means a whole way of life and not merely a few moments of ritual worship at certain prescribed times.

Jesus was born in a small town called Bethlehem nearly two thousand years ago. The fact that he was the son of God meant that no ordinary man could have been his father. Before he was born his mother Mary was visited by an angel who told her that although she was a virgin, the Holy Spirit would visit her and she would conceive and give birth to a son, to be called Jesus.

For the first thirty years of his life Jesus lived in a village called Nazareth and worked as a carpenter. The first sign that Jesus was the saviour foretold by the prophets came when he was baptized: *And when he came up out of the water, immediately he saw the heavens opened and the Spirit descending upon him like a dove; and a voice came from heaven, 'Thou art my beloved Son'* (Mark 1: 10-11). At once Jesus began to proclaim that the kingdom of of God was at hand and to call on men to repent and to believe this good news. He went through Galilee explaining what this meant by his teaching and soon gathered round him a group of disciples from among whom he chose twelve to be his constant companions.

What made Jesus so different was that he chose to spend his time preaching to the common people. He simplified his teaching by putting it in the form of stories or parables so that everyone would be able to understand. Throughout his ministry he helped the poor and the sick, assuring them of good to come: *Blessed are you poor, for yours is the kingdom of God. Blessed are you that hunger now, for you shall be satisfied. Blessed are you that weep now, for you shall laugh* (Luke 6: 20-21). He urged people to love one another and even to love their enemies: *Love your enemies, do good to those who hate you, bless those who curse you, pray for those who abuse you* (Luke 6: 27-28). He offered the way of salvation to those who would follow him and have faith. He performed miracles, healing the sick, making the blind see and cleansing lepers. He chose to mix with sinners and prostitutes and warned the rich self righteous and complacent Jews: *Woe to you that are rich, for you have received your consolation. Woe to you that are full now for you shall hunger. Woe to you that laugh now, for you shall mourn and weep* (Luke 6: 24-25).

Naturally anyone putting forward such controversial views and attracting such a following was bound to make enemies among the powerful religious leaders. Eventually Jesus was arrested on the charge of being a blasphemer. He was tried by Pontius Pilate, the Roman govenor, who could find him guilty of no real crime. This made no difference. Pilate had to give way to the hostile mob who demanded that Jesus be crucified — the punishment normally given to criminals. After being condemned to death Jesus was flogged and then forced to carry the heavy beam of the cross to the hill where he was crucified. When he was dead his disciples took the body and placed it in a stone tomb.

Two days later the body had disappeared. The stone in front of the tomb had been rolled away and all that remained inside were the bandages the body had been wrapped in. The disciples were completely bewildered until women who had followed Jesus came to tell them that an angel had reminded them of the times Jesus had said that he would rise from the dead on the third day. Some time later Jesus appeared to his disciples. At first they were terrified and thought that they were seeing a ghost but he showed them the wounds where he had been nailed to the cross and ate with them and told them that they must now go out and preach all that he had taught them. This was the last time that the disciples were to see Jesus on earth.

Jesus had been sent by God to bring new life to the teaching of the Old Testament. Before Jesus came the Jews had let their religion become a series of rites most of which had lost spiritual meaning. The religious leaders had become corrupt in their struggle for power. Jesus reminded men that to believe in God meant that they had to live in a certain way and not just offer sacrifices in the temple, go to the synagogue on the sabbath and perform certain rites at home. They must obey the Ten Commandments revealed by God to Moses (Exodus 20: 1-17). What this meant Jesus summed up very simply when he said: *You shall love the Lord your God with all your heart and with all your soul, and with all your mind. This is the great and first commandment. And a second is like it, You shall love your neighbour as yourself. On these two commandments depend all the law and the prophets* (Matthew 22: 37-40). Again, Jesus told men that they could come near to God through him. Once they believed that they could pray direct to God the ritual that had accompanied religion became less important. What mattered was that men should be truly sorry for their sins, have faith in God and try to live according to His commandments.

This means that Christians at all times should live their daily lives according to Jesus' teaching that we should love others and treat them as we would like to be treated, for example not cheat, lie, gossip or in any way just press for our own rights. It means too that the things of God, not material possessions or money, should be the most important things in life.

The Church
The word church can be used in two ways. It can mean the whole body of Christians in the world, or of one denomination, e.g. Anglican Church. It can

One of the largest of the places of worship for Christianity, the Anglican cathedral at Salisbury has a spire over a hundred metres high, the highest in Britain

also be used to describe the place where Christians worship God – a special building consecrated for the purpose, often surrounded by consecrated land where the dead can be buried.

Protestant churches differ in size and shape according to the group to which they belong. The Anglican cathedrals, whether they are old like the one at Salisbury or modern like the one at Coventry, are magnificent buildings beautifully decorated with stained glass windows and contain valuable furnishing and ornaments. At the other extreme nonconformist chapels may be small simple buildings with plain windows, whitewashed walls and a minimum of furnishing.

Worship

Formal worship takes place inside the church. In many Anglican churches there are services on weekdays but in most cases usually only on Sunday which is the day set aside for worship because it is the day on which Jesus rose from the dead. Christians are expected to attend regularly at morning or evening worship or both.

The form of church services varies within the various denominations but generally a Protestant service includes hymns, prayers, readings from the Bible and a sermon which explains a passage from the Bible and applies it to modern life. There is also an offering to maintain the church and allow it to serve those in need of help. Often the people say together the Apostles' Creed which is a simple confession of faith used since the early days of Christianity. It states:

I believe in God the Father Almighty, Maker of heaven and earth: And in Jesus Christ his only Son our Lord, Who was conceived by the Holy Ghost, Born of the Virgin Mary, Suffered under Pontius Pilate, Was crucified, dead, and buried. He descended into hell; the third day he rose again from the dead; He ascended into heaven, And sitteth on the right hand of God the Father Almighty. From thence he shall come to judge the quick and the dead. I believe in the Holy Ghost, The Holy Catholic Church, The Communion of Saints, The Forgiveness of sins, The Resurrection of the body, And the Life everlasting. Amen.

In addition to regular congregational worship all important Christian ceremonies, such as baptism, marriage and funerals, take place in church which has the added solemnity of being the house of God.

Baptism

At baptism (commonly called Christening) people are given their Christian name and become members of the Church. This can happen at any age but, apart from the Baptists, usually takes place when a child is a few months old. The parents take the child to their church where in a special service the minister pours on water, gives the child its name and blesses it 'in the name of God, the Father, the Son and the Holy Ghost'. In many cases he makes the sign of the cross on its forehead. Usually, though rarely among nonconformists, godparents (or sponsors) are present – for a boy two godfathers and one godmother; for a girl two godmothers and one godfather. These are generally relatives or close friends of the parents. They promise to take a special interest in the child, making sure that it receives religious education, and watch over its moral welfare until it grows up.

A bishop confirms a young man through the laying on of hands

Confirmation

Baptism is completed when a person decides that he is able to make for himself the vows made on his behalf by others at baptism. The ceremony is a public declaration that he has been personally converted to Christianity and wants to become a full member of the Church of Christ. The ceremony (and its name) varies from denomination to denomination. However when adult believers are concerned baptism and confirmation are a single rite.

Holy Communion

Once a person has been confirmed he becomes a communicant member of the Church and can share in the Holy Communion (Eucharist, Lord's Supper) a special service which commemorates what happened at the last supper which Jesus ate with his disciples before he was crucified: *Now as they were eating, Jesus took bread and blessed and broke it, and gave it to the disciples, and said, 'Take, eat; this is my body'. And he took a cup, and when he had given thanks he gave it to them, saying, 'Drink of it, all of you; for this is my blood of the covenant, which is poured out for mercy for the forgiveness of sins'* (Matthew 26: 26-28). Ever since Christians have obeyed Jesus' command: *Do this in remembrance of me* (1 Corinthians 11: 24). While they look back to his death for the forgiveness of their sins they know that he is present with them to enable them to live the good life and serve their fellowmen in fellowship with him. As the common term *Eucharist* signifies this is the great act of Christian thanksgiving to God for what he has done in Christ.

10

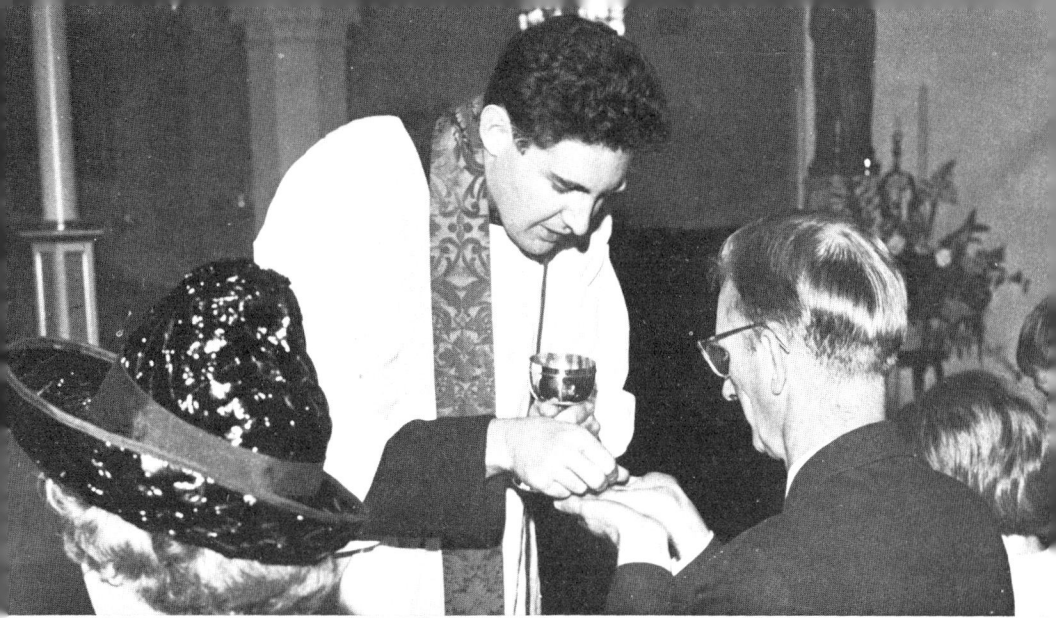

The priest gives a wafer of bread and holds the chalice containing wine at the Holy Communion service

Marriage

Christians see marriage as the life long union of a man and a woman who are joined together in the sight of God. The ceremony takes place in church and is conducted by the minister. Relatives and friends come to the service to witness the vows which the couple make. They promise to love and honour each other, to share their worldly goods and to remain faithful to one another until death.

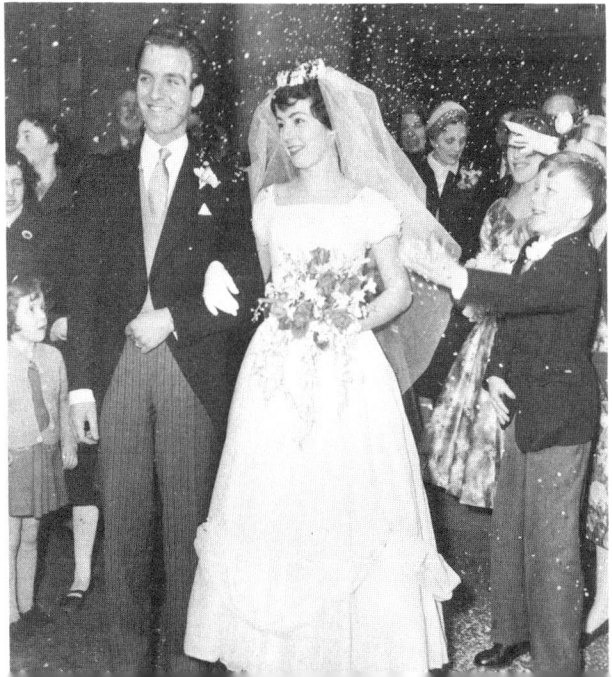

Confetti is often thrown at the end of the wedding ceremony

Burial

When a Christian dies his body is either buried in consecrated ground or cremated. Before the disposal of the body, relatives and friends attend a church service in which they are reminded of the Christian belief in life after death. Although our earthly bodies are mortal and will rot away there is a spiritual body which lives on in the presence of Christ waiting for the resurrection when God brings this world to an end. Before this comes the last judgment when Christ will deal with us according to how we have lived. So in one sense our life on earth is a preparation for the life hereafter.

Christian holidays

There are three major holidays (holy days) — Christmas, Easter and Whitsunday.

Christmas Day falls on the 25th of December and celebrates the birth of Christ. We do not know the exact date of his birth but this day, originally a pagan festival celebrating the winter solstice, was easily adopted by the Christians for this purpose. There are special services at midnight on Christmas Eve and on Christmas Day. To mark the rejoicing over God's gift of His son people give presents, send Christmas cards and decorate their houses in a special way.

Part of a burial ground where Christians' bodies are interred after death. Gravestones are usually erected as memorials

The widespread influence of Christian festivals can be seen in these illuminated decorations in London's Regent Street

Holy Week, occuring at various times in spring, celebrates the last week of Jesus' life culminating in Good Friday, the day on which he was crucified and Easter Sunday when he rose from the dead. These days are specially important for Christians. On Good Friday the churches are bare of decorations but on Easter Sunday they are fully decorated, usually with masses of white flowers. The custom of giving children easter eggs, whether of chocolate or ordinary eggs dyed in colour, is an ancient symbol of the new life given by Christ when he rose from the dead.

Whitsunday (Pentecost), six weeks after Easter, celebrates the day when the Holy Spirit came upon the disciples who were the nucleus of the first Christian Church. After Jesus had risen he appeared to his disciples and promised that when he ascended to heaven he would send them the Holy Spirit to enable them to witness to him in the world: *'But you shall receive power when the Holy Spirit has come upon you; and you shall be my witnesses in Jerusalem and in all Judea and Samaria and to the end of the earth'.... When the day of Pentecost had come, they were all together in one place. And suddenly a sound came from heaven like the rush of a mighty wind, and it filled all the house where they were sitting.... And they were all filled with the Holy Spirit* (Acts 1: 8; 2: 1-4).

2   The Protestant Reformation

The diagram shows how the Christian Church today is made up of a
number of great families. We shall try to see how the Protestant Churches
emerged from this background, why they stand for the things they do
and most important of all why they claim to belong to *the* Church.

AD
100   The Christian Church: One Holy Catholic Apostolic

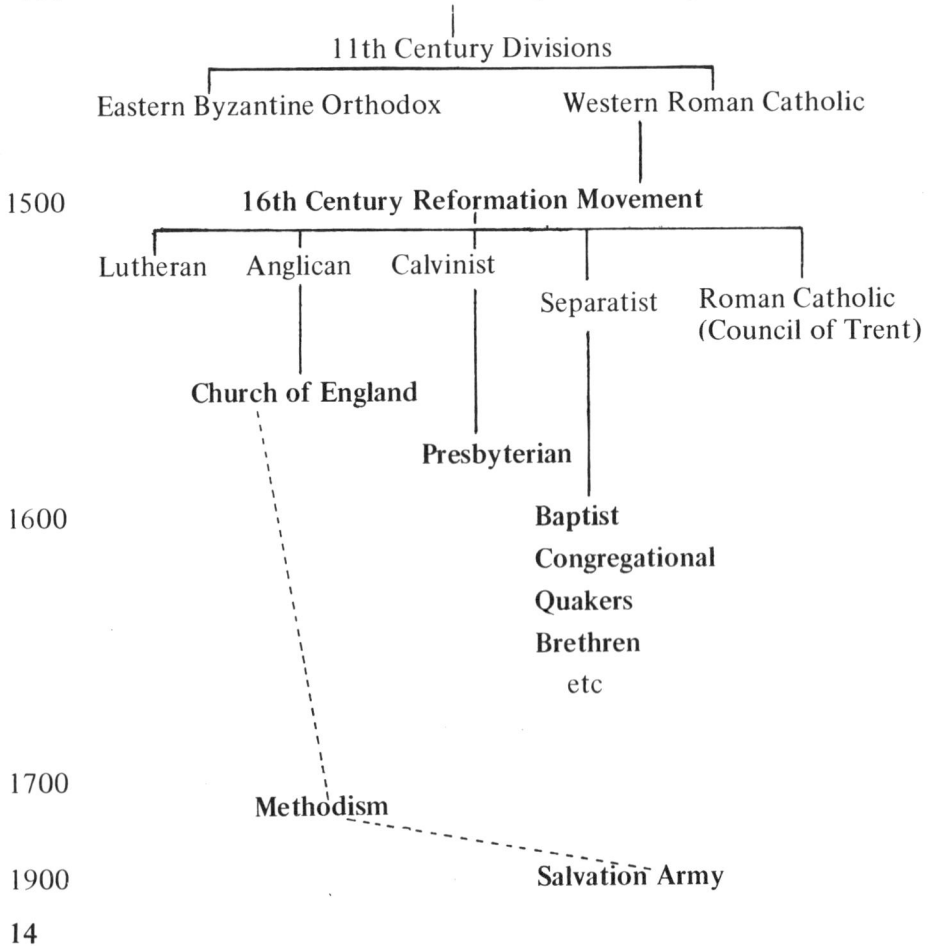

                        11th Century Divisions

       Eastern Byzantine Orthodox   Western Roman Catholic

1500   16th Century Reformation Movement

       Lutheran   Anglican   Calvinist   Roman Catholic
                                        Separatist (Council of Trent)

                   Church of England

                                Presbyterian

1600   Baptist
                                           Congregational
                                           Quakers
                                           Brethren
                                             etc

1700   Methodism

1900   Salvation Army

14

As soon as we say *Protestant* we must look at the Reformation of the sixteenth century. This reformation of the corrupt catholicism of the medieval western Church had its roots in the earlier work of Jan Hus in Bohemia and of John Wiclif in England. We shall concentrate on what happened in Germany under Martin Luther. The movement developed, as the chart shows, in three streams. The Lutheran Reformation although important in Germany, Scandinavia and later America, had only an indirect influence on our country. The second stream is important as it is the beginning of the Church of England. We shall also examine the work of John Calvin which laid the foundations of the Church of Scotland and other Presbyterian Churches.

There are other Churches stemming from those who separated from the Church of England on the grounds that the Anglican Reformation did not go far enough and who tended to the Calvinist emphasis on doctrine which we will examine later, but first what is Protestantism?

Catholic and Protestant are loaded words which have kindled much bitterness. Events in history have traditionally set them in opposition. Much of the trouble is due to the tendency to use *protest* in a negative sense. It is true that the reformers had to protest against the errors of the conditions of their time but this was because they were protesting for the truth of the Gospel. When the reformers protested against the degenerate Church of their day it was because they were protesting for the revelation through Christ and the Bible. They had to repudiate certain aspects of the Roman Church in order to affirm what they found in the word of God. They believed that a truly catholic Church must be evangelical i.e. live according to the Gospel.

Long before the Reformation, people had protested against the worldliness of the Church in the twelfth century. Later Hus in Bohemia and Wiclif in England protested against the contrast between the religion of the New Testament and that of the Church of their day. They were attempting to return to primitive simplicity and purity. They set goodness of life against mere ritual, individual freedom against ecclesiastical rules and personal conviction against formal assent. They upheld the right of a man's access to God through Christ without the intervention of the priest.

Protestantism as we understand it today is derived from the sixteenth century reformers. The movement they led is the most momentous Christian event since the conversion of the Roman Empire in the fourth century. Broadly speaking it was a successful revolt against the power of the western Church under the Pope at Rome which embraced the Christians of Europe claiming to meet all the needs of men and society. It may have compromised with the weakness of the common man, but it provided in monasticism a way of holiness for those wishing to be perfect. Its system of sacraments (the rites of the Christian Church, in particular baptism and Holy Communion) offered the grace of God to all. It also supervised education and culture.

However, from the end of the middle ages it was generally agreed that the whole structure was due for a radical overhaul. Most people felt that stricter discipline would deal with practical abuses and the main pattern could be left untouched. Others saw that the trouble went deeper. Christianity seemed to have become identified with a vast paraphernalia of rites. There were many evils inherent in the system itself and in particular bound up with a materialistic understanding of the sacraments.

We can single out one issue to illustrate the state of the Church at the beginning of the sixteenth century, the *Interdict.* This was an order which the Pope could issue against a town or even a whole country which had offended him. The Interdict prevented priests from giving the sacraments. This meant that people could not be married, children could not be baptized and no one could take Holy Communion while it lasted.

Martin Luther

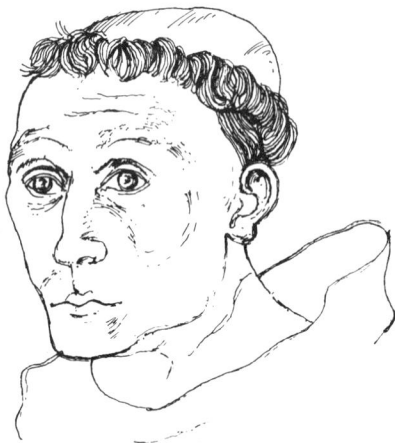

Martin Luther used this issue to begin his protest. In 1517 he published 95 Theses condemning practices associated with the sale of Indulgences (these were pieces of paper which granted forgiveness of sins). The suggestion that a man could buy forgiveness for his sins with cash provoked Luther's anger. He was not attacking the Church in general but this protest against one abuse provoked criticism of the whole system in the minds of some Christians. Many, even among those who agreed that there were things to put right, jumped to the conclusion that the whole divine authority of the Church was in danger and by treating what began as a simple plea for one reform as though it were a general revolt they helped to make it such.

During the ensuing conflict between what we may call the radical and the conservative groups two ideas began to emerge which were to be fundamental to Protestantism: firstly that there can be churchmanship other than that under the Papacy, and secondly the idea that the word of God revealed in the scriptures is the standard for Christian faith and practice. In this way the movement developed as an appeal to the revealed will of God against the corruptions infecting the Church. The Reformers abolished many holy days in order to give prominence to Advent, Easter and Pentecost and to make Sunday unrivalled. They pruned the accessories from worship in order to bring the Bible and sacraments into prominence. They agreed that there are many holy rites but none to compare with baptism and Holy Communion. In the latter they removed all details which did not relate to the Lord's Supper in order to stress the important factors. Recognizing man's need for a heavenly mediator they encouraged him to turn to Christ alone and offer his prayers through him. They rejected the idea that only a priest or monk can be fully obedient to God and taught that men living in the world could live a full Christian life. The result was a total change in the structure of the western Church. It was not so much reformed as fragmented. A number of separated Churches came into being each with its own confession of faith and all broadly named Protestant or Evangelical.

This word was originally given to the followers of Luther's evangelical doctrines but was soon extended to all who accepted the principles of the Protestant Reformation. This meant severance from Rome but Protestantism is not simply non Romanism. Protestants regard their main doctrines as true – not merely as non Roman or anti Roman. Nor should we forget the common area of belief and practice which is simply Christian.

We can say very broadly, that the sixteenth century reformers challenged the Church of their day on the following main issues:

1 The Pope as vicar of Christ and the claim that there was no salvation outside the Church of which he is head.
2 Maintaining Church tradition to be equal or even superior to scripture as the basis of doctrine.
3 Discouraging ordinary people from reading the Bible in their own language.
4 The doctrine of transubstantiation and communion in one kind i.e. the people only being given bread during Holy Communion.
5 The number of the sacraments – seven or two.
6 Compulsory celibacy of the clergy.
7 The doctrine of purgatory and the practice of saying prayers for the dead.
8 Worshipping the saints, especially the Virgin Mary.
9 The powers of the priesthood, a problem made more difficult by the fact that so many priests were corrupt.

Bound up with these religious issues were many non theological factors including the revolutionary effects of the Renaissance and the new emphasis on the rights of the individual, the development of European states resentful of the claims of the Papacy and fired with a new spirit of nationalism, and the fact that the Church had enormous wealth often grossly misused.

There can be no doubt that reform was needed; the only criticisms concern the manner in which it was carried out and the divisions to which it led. The previous great schism in the eleventh century between western Catholicism and eastern Orthodoxy bitter as it was, at least meant that for most Christians there was only one Church where they lived. The Reformation fragmented the western Church in all directions; now in large areas of the world the Church of Christ has been split into groups, often several in one place, each challenging the right of the others to be the Churoh or even to be Christian.

Reformation can be used to describe a complicated series of changes in the west going back as far as the criticism of the medieval Church by the Lollards in England and the Hussites in Bohemia. For our purposes we shall begin with Martin Luther in Germany and his fresh discovery of Christianity according to St Paul. A monk obsessed with sin (John Osborne's play will give you an idea of his personality) he came to see in the word of God (both as incarnate in Jesus Christ and as written in the Bible) the miracle of God's love bestowing a forgiveness which could not be earned but only received as a gift. This is the doctrine of justification by grace through faith which is at the heart of Reformation theology. It means that when a man puts his faith in Jesus Christ as his saviour he is set free from all that is merely legal in order to become the means to convey the love of God to his neighbour. It was just because he believed this that Luther had to protest against the system of Indulgences and to accept the consequences of his protest.

At first it was a purely religious matter. Luther had no idea or desire of separating from the Papacy, still less of having a Church bearing his name. When in 1517 he focussed his protest on abuses connected with the Church's system of penance he was not really breaking new ground; earlier reformers had shown that deep personal faith did not necessarily conflict with the Church as an institution. Had it been only a matter of the 95 Theses there might well have been a revival but almost certainly no schism. When Luther went on to question the medieval emphasis on good works as the way to salvation and to query the papal claim to absolute supremacy it was another matter. He attacked the doctrine that bread and wine were transubstantiated into the actual body and blood of Christ during Holy Communion and called for reform of the religious orders and abolition of papal power in Germany.

By supporting the German princes in the peasants' revolt, Luther gained their help, and later that of the Kings of Denmark and Sweden. In 1530 the reforming beliefs were summed up in the *Augsburg Confession* and by the time Luther died in 1546 the Protestant Churches in Germany and Scandinavia which had followed his pattern of reformation were all state Churches under the control of the local ruler.

The main beliefs of the Protestant Reformation are contained in the confessions, traditions, worship and life of a great community of more than 200 millions with a history of over four centuries. The Reformation emphasis on spiritual freedom rather than the Church dictating what a man must believe and do, can and does lead to exaggeration of the right of private judgment which helps to explain the many sects within Protestant Christianity in striking contrast to the monolithic character of the Roman Church.

The vast majority of Protestants, probably over ninety per cent, are to be found in the six main communions: Lutheran, Anglican, Presbyterian, Baptist, Congregational and Methodist. Of Lutheranism we need say no more as it plays only a small part in the British scene, but the others play a very large part in the story of Britain and its influence overseas.

3   The Church of England

In the summer of 1968 a great conference was held at Lambeth Palace, the London home of the Archbishop of Canterbury. There has been a series of these Lambeth Conferences when hundreds of bishops representing nine million Christians all over the world are able to meet united in their common relationship with Canterbury, the mother church founded in 597 by Augustine, a missionary sent by Pope Gregory the Great.

There had been Christians in Britain during Roman times but after the Teutonic conquests early British Christianity remained only among the Celts of Cornwall, Wales and Ireland. For a long time it had little influence among the pagan conquerors but at about the time Augustine came to Kent, Celtic missionaries from the monastery established in Iona began to work in the north. So two independent and somewhat hostile missions worked for the conversion of England until it was agreed at the Synod of Whitby in 664 that British Christianity should be Roman not Celtic. So up until the Reformation the British Church along with the rest of western Europe was in full communion with the Pope. But just as the kingdom was never regarded as part of the Holy Roman Empire, the Church maintained some independence and the Archbishop of Canterbury was never as subordinate to the Papacy as the continental archbishops.

Lambeth Palace, conference centre for the Anglican Church and residence of the Archbishop of Canterbury

From the thirteenth century there was strong national feeling in England against the Papacy, not only among the heretical Lollards ('Prayer mumblers' – followers of John Wiclif, who based their teaching on the Bible and personal faith and were strongly critical of much in the Church as an institution especially its power and wealth) but generally, and antipapal laws were enacted. The same period saw the development of the parochial system based on the idea that each local community should include a priest, the person or parson who made a special contribution to its life. This has continued to be an important element in the Anglican tradition and explains why the vicar or rector is still regarded as minister of the whole parish and not simply of his own congregation.

The English Church from the fifteenth century onwards could not but be influenced by movements and events on the continent yet its own Reformation had special causes and took an independent line. Henry VIII had little sympathy with Luther. It was his book criticizing Luther's views which led the Pope to grant him the title 'Defender of the Faith' which is represented by the initials FID DEF on our coins.

In the background however things were stirring. The Lollards had been suppressed but their tradition continued in the widespread anticlerical feeling. Erasmus, the great European scholar whose satires on the doctrines and institutions of the Church paved the way for the Reformation, had a great influence on Dean Colet of St Paul's Cathedral and Sir Thomas More. Together they encouraged liberal Renaissance ideas. As the State grew more strongly organized it began to create nationalist sentiment. All in all, it was likely that any break between Pope and King would be followed by the separation of the Church from the Papacy and this is exactly what happened. Whereas on the Continent the religious movement became political, it was a political matter in England which led to the ecclesiastical separation.

Things came to a head because of the King's divorce. Henry was married to Katherine of Aragon who failed to give him the male heir so vital to the realm. A decree of nullity would have been the simple answer but Katherine refused this on religious grounds. Determined to marry Anne Boleyn, the King turned for help to the English Parliament. Conscious of its strength and glad to give expression to its anticlerical views, it passed acts forbidding Church courts to appeal to Rome and declared the King to be the only supreme head on earth of the Church of England. This meant the end of the Pope's authority in England. When Cranmer became Archbishop of Canterbury his first act was to declare the marriage null and void.

Henry proceeded to use his new ecclesiastical authority to attack the monasteries because he felt they were too close to the Papacy and no longer had any positive value. He also needed their wealth. When the dissolution of the monasteries was completed in 1540 some abbeys became parish churches and some of the money was used to found new dioceses, but most of it passed to men who had their own interest in this kind of reformation.

More positive was the order in 1538 to put an English version of the Bible in every parish church. This was the Great Bible based on the translation by Tyndale, a radical Protestant who had been burned as a heretic in Brussels in 1536. The people thronged to hear the Bible read and came to recognize an authority other than that of the priest. Thus the way was opened for theological discussion and argument.

However by the time of Henry's death, reformation had not gone far. The Papacy still existed but without the Pope. The King had assumed quasi papal authority over the Church but with the exception of the monasteries the old pattern continued. The basic Reformation teaching of Luther had made little headway. Reforms were limited to putting the Bible and worship into English with some check on superstitious worship of the saints. There was little desire among English churchmen to alter radically the old catholic system.

When Henry was succeeded by Edward VI the court, supported by Cranmer, seemed ready for greater change. Cranmer's translation of the Prayer Book begun under Henry was issued in 1549 for general compulsory use. The Mass was now Holy Communion and all were expected to take both bread and wine. The translation made for simplicity and eliminated the possibilities of superstition. Its use allowed the worshippers to be active participants rather than passive spectators but its interpretation still made the doctrine of transubstantiation possible. With the help of Protestant scholars from the Continent, a second Prayer Book in which the Reformation note was stronger was published in 1552.

In 1553 Edward was succeeded by Katherine's daughter Mary, a pious and intelligent woman. Embittered by her mother's experience, she sought to vindicate her name by reversing Henry's policy. Needing a male heir she married Philip, son of Emperor Charles V. It was an unpopular move for it

John Wiclif

A Protestant woman locked in a cage on London Bridge during Papist repression in Mary's reign

brought the nation within the orbit of the Holy Roman Empire. Nevertheless Parliament agreed to repeal the ecclesiastical legislation. In 1555 England was reconciled with the Papacy and Cranmer was burned as a heretic. Mary and her cousin Cardinal Pole, made archbishop in 1557, began persecution and the martyrs were mostly simple Christians whose courage and sincerity led to bitter reaction against Mary and her religion.

She died in 1558, a childless failure, and was succeeded by Elizabeth I who was proud of being the daughter of Henry VIII. It was probably her own wish to let the old religion go on without the Pope but events moved fast and she was pressed by returning Protestant exiles to make radical changes. In 1559 the Act of Supremacy again separated England from the Papacy but Elizabeth did not assume the title of supreme head. Also in 1559 the Act of Uniformity prescribed the second Prayer Book of 1552 for general use.

Many of the bishops appointed by Mary resigned rather than accept this settlement. This made the matter of episcopal succession difficult. Matthew Parker, a moderate reformer, was chosen to be archbishop and was consecrated by four bishops of the reign of Edward VI. He joined them in consecrating bishops for the vacancies. So in spite of Roman Catholic refusal to acknowledge the fact, the ministerial continuity of the English Church was maintained.

23

Elizabeth wanted a Church which allowed room for all shades of opinion and so in 1571 she ratified the 39 Articles of Religion, the most comprehensive of all the confessions of the Reformation Churches which allowed for reasonable difference of opinion on all matters under dispute. There were some who strongly urged further reform on Calvinist lines but Elizabeth stood firm.

In this way the break with Rome begun in 1529 was completed in Elizabeth's reign. There were however some who continued to be loyal to the Pope in spite of laws to the contrary. For a while they continued to be in communion with the majority but in 1570 the Pope settled matters by forbidding them to worship in the parish churches.

By the end of the sixteenth century the Church of England had become very much what it is today. The main effect of the Reformation was to reject the authority of the Papacy for that of the crown. The precise relationship has never been clearly defined but it is understood that the sovereign works in harmony with the representatives of the Church in such a way as to make an 'Established' Church. The historic episcopate, however, was maintained.

On the positive side the Reformation gave people the Bible and the Book of Common Prayer in their own tongue. This was a matter of tremendous importance as there is no Church which gives greater prominence to the reading of the Bible in public worship.

The term Establishment which describes the peculiar relationship of Church to State in England does not mean that the State created, governs or provides for the Church. In fact Anglicans are less under the authority of the State than many Lutherans. This is due in part to the English tradition of political freedom and in part to the authority exercised by the episcopate. The continuing existence of dissenting minorities demonstrates that membership of the State does not entail membership of the Church. The Establishment is a matter of mutual recognition and obligation, as illustrated by the Convocations of Canterbury and York. These are legislative bodies who have the same right of access to the sovereign as Parliament. It means that the State confesses the Christian faith and is pledged to maintain and defend it. The high conception of the nature and responsibilities of both Church and State is symbolized in the coronation where the role of the Church stresses the sanctity of the sovereign's office.

Of course, the overseas provinces and daughter churches within the Anglican communion have never been established and the recent disestablishment of the Church in Ireland and Wales leaves the Church of England alone established. Its governing body, the National Assembly, is composed of the upper and lower houses i.e. bishops and clergy respectively of the Convocations of Canterbury and York, along with a house of representative laity, under the chairmanship of the Archbishop of Canterbury. The Assembly meets in London three times a year mainly to prepare ecclesiastical measures for Parliament.

Clearly the English Reformation was very different from any of the continental forms. It was the most conservative of all the sixteenth century separations from Rome. In a typically English way it sought to purify the old religion by appeal to scripture and the early Christian writers. It renounced nothing that was regarded as essential to catholic Christianity. For example, the practice of invoking the saints in prayer was rejected but the due observance of saints' days was retained. The great concern was to maintain that the Church of England is *the* Catholic Church in England.

There was little continental influence until the reign of Edward VI when long exhortations in the Lutheran manner were inserted into the Prayer Book. This, first published in 1549 and revised in 1552, 1559 and 1662, became both the basis and heart of Anglican life and worship. The 1662 Book of Common Prayer is still widely used.

Before going on to describe the Anglicanism of today we must look again at history in order to set the context in which the other Churches we are to consider begin to emerge.

In the seventeenth century, the majority of English Christians were happy with the Elizabethan settlement and the greatly loved Prayer Book services but there was a continuing Roman minority and others who wished that Elizabeth had allowed reform to go further. These Puritans were not content merely to be tolerated, they wanted to reshape the English Church on Calvinist lines. Other minority groups emerged including the Brownists or Independents, forerunners of later Congregationalism, who stressed the local congregation as the New Testament pattern of churchmanship and the Baptists who thought people should be baptized when they were adult and not as children. To understand the significance of these minority movements we need to examine some broad historical outlines.

When James VI of Scotland succeeded Elizabeth as James I of England the Puritans hoped that as he had been reared in Scotland, which had followed the Calvinist Reformation, he would be prepared to modify the Settlement according to their ideas. But James, although Calvinist in doctrine, had seen enough of Presbyterianism in action. He realised that the English way of episcopal government was more favourable to the king's position. At the Hampton Court conference of 1604 he met the Puritan demands with 'No bishop, no king'.

This tendency developed under Charles I who favoured the new school of theologians with their high views of the Church as an institution and of the

A Puritan lady

function of the clergy rather than those who stressed personal religion and minimized the difference between clergy and laity.

In the Civil War 1642–49, the issue between King and Parliament was constitutional, but the choice of sides tended to be on religious grounds. The loyalist high churchmen who supported the king in his view of divine right wanted no change in the Settlement. They were opposed by the Puritans of Parliament and most of the public who did.

When Charles was executed in 1649 the power remained with Cromwell and the army which was composed largely of Independents and Baptists. So the reform of the English Church was not simply on Presbyterian lines. Under the Commonwealth, Anglicans lost political rights and were forbidden to use the Prayer Book in public worship. Clergymen who persisted in doing so were ejected. The Puritans, who had seemed to many to have been unjustly deprived of freedom under Anglican rule, became even more intolerant when in power. Hence there was a reaction in favour of the Anglicans and after the Restoration of 1660 the balance was more than restored.

In 1661 bishops and Presbyterian leaders met at the Savoy Conference to consider the revision of the Prayer Book and to see if there could be a place for Presbyterians in the English Church. They failed to reach agreement and a year later the Act of Uniformity declared the amended (1662) Prayer Book to be the only form for public worship. Clergy unwilling to accept this were ejected. They gathered congregations around them under the name of Protestant Dissenters.

From this time the Puritans had no hope of changing the Church of England. In their dissenting chapels they had freedom from State control but they were to suffer under intolerant laws. Some relief was to come to

26

them in a curious way. James II was a Roman Catholic. In an attempt to restore the old religion he ordered the suspension of the penal laws against non Anglicans. The seven bishops who in 1688 led a petition against this were charged with sedition but acquitted. About the same time, the unexpected arrival of a male heir to the throne gave the prospect of a Roman Catholic dynasty. The heir presumptive had been Mary, James' daughter by a previous marriage, an Anglican married to the Calvinist Prince William of Orange. When James fled friendless to France, Parliament offered the crown jointly to William and Mary. The revolution had certain effects. It ensured that no Roman Catholic or one married to such could sit on the English throne. Further, the dissenters who supported the Anglicans against the Roman threat were permitted by the Toleration Act to worship as they chose in their own chapels although political restrictions were not removed until 1828 and privileges in the universities were withheld even longer.

Many high church Anglicans were conscientiously unable to accept William and Mary while James lived. The bishops involved had to resign as they could not take the oath of allegiance.

One condition of the union of the kingdoms of England and Scotland in 1707 was the establishment of Presbyterianism as the Church of Scotland. The sovereign becomes a Presbyterian on crossing the border. In addition to a number who had remained Roman Catholic all along there was a minority who could not accept this arrangement and they became organized as the Episcopal Church of Scotland.

In the eighteenth century a new movement developed in the Church of England. It was hostile to both high and low traditions but lacking the values of either it had a low spiritual life. It was partly in reaction to this that the evangelical movement and the separation of the Methodists grew.

The Evangelical Revival was little concerned with intellectual, liturgical and institutional matters but laid great stress on personal devotion to Christ and the practical application of Christianity. The Evangelicals strongly supported the struggle to end slavery and did much to remind the Church of its missionary obligation and were behind movements such as those leading to the founding of the Bible Society.

The Catholic Revival of the Oxford Movement was complementary to that of the Evangelicals. It sought to arrest the moral and spiritual decline by a return to the high church ideals of the seventeenth century. This involved stressing that the Church of England was *the* Church in England with the Prayer Book as its rule of faith. The movement had great influence in restoring dignity and beauty to worship and authority to the ministry, especially the bishops. One effect was to reintroduce religious communities of monks and nuns.

In spite of these crises the Church of England has maintained its integrity and character as a comprehensive Church. This is due to the fact that the English Reformation was more moderate and less radical than others. Wanting to preserve as much as possible of what was good in the past, especially in matters of Church order and worship it took a middle path between Rome and the extreme Protestantism of the Continent. The English reformers, seeking to continue in England the tradition of the undivided Church of the past four centuries repudiated what they regarded as Roman corruptions while holding on to much that the continental reformers rejected.

Anglican theology manages to keep a balance between the Catholic and Protestant elements. If we can single out one typically Anglican feature it is perhaps the emphasis on Jesus Christ, the Son of God made man where others might stress the fact that he died for our sins.

It is difficult to pinpoint Anglicanism and set it out in clear categories.

Evidence of what all Anglicans regard as essential can be found in their view of what is necessary as a basis for reunion. The *Appeal to all Christian people* from the Lambeth Conference 1920 included the famous Quadrilateral:

1 The Holy Scriptures of the Old and New Testaments contain all things necessary for salvation and are the rule and ultimate standard of faith.
2 The Apostles' Creed as the baptismal symbol and the Nicene Creed are a sufficient statement of the Christian faith.
3 The two sacraments ordained by Christ himself — baptism and the Lord's Supper — should be ministered with unfailing use of Christ's words and the elements ordained by him.
4 The historic episcopate should be adapted to the varying needs of the nations and peoples called by God into the unity of His Church.

Today the Church of England has about 18,000 churches most of them easily distinguished by the square tower or lofty spire outside and inside by the long nave directing attention to the sanctuary with the altar at the east end. There are roughly the same number of ordained ministers, bishops, priests and deacons. The characteristic dress is cassock, surplice and scarf or stole. An increasing number wear eucharistic vestments for Holy Communion.

It is by far the largest Church in England with at least three fifths of the population nominally Anglican. Marriages provide a useful standard of reference; 50 per cent take place in Anglican churches; 12 per cent in Roman Catholic; 10 per cent in the various Free Churches and the rest in Registry Offices. So although the Church of England is the national Church it is not that of all the people as is the Church of Sweden.

The Church of England is divided into dioceses, each governed within by a bishop, which are grouped with the two provinces of Canterbury and York, each under the jurisdiction of an archbishop. The dioceses are subdivided into

St Giles Church, Camberwell, a typical C of E church with a long high nave leading to the altar at the east end

rural deaneries which are groups of parishes in the charge of a senior clergyman called the rural dean. Each parish has a council elected annually and is due to meet at least four times a year. The considerable revenues and estates of the Church are managed by commissioners. At every level of church government an increasing part is being given to the layman.

In the eighteenth and nineteenth centuries the Church of England expanded rapidly throughout the world. This was due in part to colonial expansion and the success of the Church in following the flag. The Anglican churches in what were once colonies but are now self governing nations e.g. Canada, Australia, New Zealand, West Indies, South Africa, are now independent of, but in full communion with, the mother church. It was due also to the activity of the missionary societies. Throughout Asia, Africa and Latin America, missionary bishoprics were set up under the jurisdiction of Canterbury. Most of these have become independent indigenous Churches but linked with the others mentioned above by the Lambeth Conference. This meets approximately every ten years under the presidency of the Archbishop of Canterbury and is attended by all Anglican bishops. It is a consultative body with no executive authority, but its reports and advice have great weight and it is an important bond of union between Churches the world over which can trace common ancestry to the English Reformation and whose faith and order are controlled by Prayer Books modelled on that of 1662.

4   The Presbyterian Churches

The Lutheran Reformation had its main success in Germany and Scandinavia. Elsewhere Protestant teaching advanced in the more definite and militant Calvinist form. This led to setting up Reformed (Presbyterian) Churches in Switzerland, France, the Netherlands and Scotland.

When Luther's evangelical teaching reached France it was welcomed by the learned circle around the king's sister, Margaret of Valois. This ensured toleration for the new views and brought John Calvin, born in Picardy, into early contact with Lutheranism. He studied theology in Paris but was never ordained priest. In 1553 he became a Protestant and fleeing from France in fear of persecution, set to work on his *Institutes of the Christian Religion.* Published in 1536 this gave Protestantism the systematic theology it so far lacked and confronted the Roman Catholics with a creed as rigorously articulated and a government as closely organized as their own.

The main doctrines of Calvinism can be summed up briefly and concisely:
1 The Bible is the sole basis of the Christian faith. Here lies all Christian truth. Church tradition and the decisions of the ecumenical councils have no authority unless shown to be based on scripture.
2 While agreeing with Luther on justification by faith, Calvin began not with personal experience of forgiveness but with an overwhelming sense of the greatness and majesty of God.
3 All creation is absolutely dependent on God. All that happens is preordained. There is human freedom but it is subject to the overuling of divine providence.
4 In line with Augustine and Luther, Calvin stressed the total depravity and corruption of human nature.
5 All men deserve to be damned but God has predestined some to be saved – these are the elect. For all others God has preordained eternal damnation. Christ died for the salvation only of the elect, not for all. Nevertheless the Gospel must be preached to all.
6 Augustine had held that it was possible for a man to fall from grace, but Calvin's doctrine of final perseverance (i.e. continuance in a state of grace to the end) declared that God's purpose in election could not fail. He linked the regeneration or rebirth of the elect not with baptism but with the knowledge of being among the elect and so assured of salvation. Baptism

is the sign or seal by which the child of Christian parents is brought into relation with God.

By choosing a form of church government by presbyters rather than bishops, Calvinism claimed to be a reformation on the New Testament pattern. According to Calvin the only legitimate church order is that found in the New Testament where bishop (overseer) and presbyter (elder) are synonymous. All denominations agree on this point. Where Calvin differed was in his conclusion that the Church ought therefore always to be governed by a council of presbyters. In his system each congregation is presided over by a council of ruling elders with a minister trained and ordained for preaching and administration of the sacraments. He alone is full time and paid. The others are members who earn their living in secular work but are ordained as elders to assist the minister in matters of organization and discipline. For this reason Churches reformed on the Calvinist pattern are called Presbyterian.

The Lutherans tended to make no distinction between Church and State, but Calvin claimed the same freedom from State control as had been enjoyed by the medieval Papacy. So while the Lutherans tended to be politically conservative, the Calvinists were often behind revolutionary nationalist movements. The democratic presbyterian organization of the churches made them training grounds for democracy.

Calvin stressed discipline (literally the way of the disciple). His determination to restore the authority which the Church exercised over the members in New Testament days helped to counteract the tendency of some Protestants to think that if salvation was in the hands of God, what men did was unimportant. He refused to recognize a double moral standard—one for

John Calvin

the holy and another for the common man. He rejected the pattern of medieval asceticism and attached no special value to celibacy as opposed to marriage. Rather he demanded of all Christians standards which had never been attempted since the earliest days such as abstinence from all kinds of simple pleasure, dancing, drama, music, gay clothing. This is the aspect of Calvinism commonly called Puritanism which has had much influence on the Christian tradition in Britain. It stems from the belief that the natural impulses of fallen men are sinful and calls for complete self control. Its influence tends to make worship plain, austere and colourless.

When Calvin was called to organize the Protestants in Geneva his views proved too stern to be acceptable and he was expelled. But he was soon recalled and from 1541 to his death in 1564 he had considerable influence. He used the civil courts to enforce the discipline of the Church which he so organized as to make Geneva the heart of the Protestant world. Calvinism spread over Europe to form national Churches in Holland and Scotland and set up smaller but influential groups elsewhere.

All the Churches which trace their origin to the Calvinist form of reformation have a family resemblance. This is not simply the common form of Presbyterian church order. It includes a characteristic type of doctrine, ritual and behaviour which, despite modification and development down the years and in different areas, still expresses Calvin's tendency to reject everything not found in the New Testament as being popish. In worship they use hymns, especially the psalms, but for a long time they had no organ.

The churches are dignified but plain, with great emphasis given to the pulpit. At Holy Communion, the congregation is seated around the table which replaces the altar. Ministers wear the black scholar's gown with white neck bands. Great stress is laid on the sermon and spontaneous prayer.

The oldest and largest Presbyterian Church in Britain is the national Church of Scotland. There were Christians in Scotland from the fourth century. By the sixteenth century the Church had become so corrupt that reforming influences from the continent were warmly welcomed but this took a different form from those in England. It began as a popular religious movement and had a long struggle with the authorities before taking shape as the Church of Scotland at the end of the seventeenth century.

The Scots were first influenced by Luther's teaching but under the powerful teaching of John Knox, a disciple of Calvin, they gradually opted for the Genevan form of doctrine and order. Soon the nobles too began to support the evangelical movement and eventually after a general attack on the old churches and monasteries, Parliament came on to the reforming side in 1560. When the crown of England and Scotland were united King James

The simplicity of the Presbyterian Church at Hartley, near Plymouth, contrasts with the more ornate style of C of E churches such as that shown on page 29

attempted to force the Establishment upon Scotland. Nobility, ministers and people joined in a new covenant to protect their faith against the English Church.

In the early days of the revolution in England, the Presbyterians were in power and tried to establish Presbyterianism generally. They produced certain documents which became the basis of the Presbyterian Church established in 1688 as the Church of Scotland.

From the eighteenth century several Free Churches came into being and in 1843 about a third seceded to form the Free Church of Scotland. After a time the separations began to break down and there have been many reunions though in each case a stubborn minority remained apart. The most important union was in 1929 when the great majority of Scottish Presbyterians came together and drew up a constitution guaranteeing national recognition of religion and the spiritual independence of the Church.

For Presbyterians the most important guide in life is the word of God and this is reflected in the simple, orderly, dignified pattern of Presbyterian worship with its traditional emphasis on preaching.

Presbyterian belief has been influenced by modern society, in particular there is less importance given to the belief that only certain chosen people will be saved. The Presbyterians in the USA have removed certain clauses which separate the non elect from the love of God and added new sections stressing the work of the Holy Spirit, the universal love of God and the duty of the Church to go into all the world to make disciples.

Presbyterian views on the government of the Church are especially concerned with preserving spiritual freedom, particularly with regard to the Church's freedom to govern itself according to what it believes to be the will of God. Under the sole authority of Christ as King and Head, church government is carried out through selected offices.

The Presbyterian Church of England is governed by representative councils of ministers and elders. The supreme court is the General Assembly presided over by a moderator who is elected annually. The local Presbytery has oversight of all the congregations and ministers in its area. Each congregation has its representatives in both courts which aim to encourage, guide and correct pastoral work. In this way all the members have rights and responsibilities for the life of their church. The congregations elect elders to share authority with the minister and to help him in pastoral care.

The Church court decides all matters concerned with doctrine and worship. This emphasis on the spiritual independence of the Church which means its duty is to obey God rather than man, had made Presbyterians prominent in struggles for freedom. Yet they also recognize that the State itself is a divine society with an authority of its own which can be used to glorify God. All this has made Presbyterians solid and stable members of society.

Presbyterianism has been carried far by missionaries, travellers, traders and colonists. It is strong in Australia, Canada, New Zealand and, of course, in the USA where Presbyterianism has made its mark on the course of history and the shaping of the Constitution. Nearer home is the Presbyterian Church of Ireland founded in 1642, and the Presbyterian Church of Wales.

The alliance of Reformed Churches which represents Presbyterian Churches has nearly twelve million members. The present Presbyterian Church of England has over 300 churches and ministers.

5   The Separatist Protestant Churches

We use this term to cover several kinds of Reformed Churches which all believe that the local congregation should be the primary unit of the Church. This is based on what men understood from the New Testament. People set up voluntary societies which tended to follow the Calvinist pattern of doctrine and worship. The people who formed them were not content with the Church of England Reformation. The best known among these are the Congregationalists, the Baptists and some smaller groups such as the Society of Friends (known often as Quakers) and the Brethren.

Congregational
Congregationalists believe that the local congregation forms the Church which has Christ as its sole head. Where two or three people are met in Christ's name, he is in their midst to guide thought and inspire action. Each congregation gathered together is regarded as the local expression of the universal Church. There are no popes, bishops or kings – only Christ reigns supreme. Such a doctrine calls for high standards of devotion and Congregationalists are the first to admit that in practice they often fail to rise to them.

When the Church of England separated from Rome there were many who considered that the reforms had not gone far enough and a great deal of corruption remained under the Establishment. As early as 1550 there were Christians in England meeting to preach and administer the sacraments quite separate from the national Church. These groups increased under the leadership of Robert Browne. These Brownists gathered together in local congregations to try to find purer forms of worship and to be independent of the State. Although they emphasized the local congregation as the unit of organization, they were not primarily interested in Church order. They regarded the life of the Church as centred in the Bible, the sacraments and godly discipline.

The Brownists grew in the face of persecution and as more and more congregations were founded the movement took shape as Congregationalism. When it was driven underground in England, many of these nonconforming Christians fled to Holland. From here one group sailed to America in a boat called the *Mayflower* and established a colony in New England in 1620, which played a large part in shaping religion and politics in America.

Yet even under persecution the movement continued in England. Many Independents became leaders in Cromwell's struggle with Charles I, and formed the backbone of his army. When the Westminster Assembly met to reform the English Church there were delegates to plead the cause of Independency. The Acts of Uniformity made the Congregationalists 'nonconformists' but later the Toleration Act gave them the right to exist.

The Congregationalists continued to grow in number and influence. When excluded from the universities they built strong Dissenting Academies which were to play a part in founding the University of London.

We still have to speak of Congregational churches for the principle of independency maintains belief in the New Testament teaching that each local congregation is the embodiment of the universal Church. Yet though independent, the Congregational churches are less and less isolated. The recognition of a bond of common faith and order and the principle that the strong must help the weak has led to congregations joining together for mutual help and to speak on public issues with one voice. Each local congregation is free to choose its own minister. There is no special dress for the minister. He may wear a clerical collar but many choose not to do so. The sense of the priesthood of all believers is so strong that they do not wish in any way to be distinguished from other members of the congregation. When conducting worship most ministers wear academic robes or a black gown with or without white bands. Members of the congregation also appoint lay officials called deacons who lead and organize church life.

Congregationalists are often accused of having no creed. It is true that they refuse to impose any formula as a test of membership. They believe that written definitions of faith coming down from the past may hinder obedience to the teaching of the Holy Spirit in the present time but they do regard the historic Creeds and the Reformation Confessions as useful declarations of the Christian faith and would reckon to live by their principles and in harmony with their spirit.

At present there are nearly 3,000 churches and about 1,700 ordained ministers.

Baptist

The persecution of the English Nonconformists drove many of the separatists overseas, especially to Holland where there was full freedom for the various Reformation groups. In Amsterdam a group emerged which believed that the local congregation was the basic unit of the Church. Like the Congregationalists they met in congregation for worship and mutual help but they were unique in baptizing only adult believers according to what they saw to be the clear teaching and method of the New Testament. This involves being completely submerged beneath the water, as happened in the time that Jesus lived. The people would gather on the banks of a river and when they were baptized they would be pushed bodily under the water as a sign of dying to their former sinful life. When they emerged it symbolized the beginning of their new way of life.

The Baptists as we know them today originated from the Reformed Protestant tradition through the refugee separatists from England early in the seventeenth century. John Smyth, a separatist exile in Holland, in 1609 declared that members of the congregation had to be baptized and members of Smyth's group returned to London in 1612 to set up a Church. The Baptist congregations which grew rapidly in England were very close to the Independents for a while but in 1664 they separated on the issue of immersion. Along with other Nonconformists they were oppressed till the end of the century, as were those who in 1639 had gone to America. Nevertheless they spread and today Baptists are found all over the world and form one of the largest Protestant Churches with nearly twenty million members and over fifty million in the community.

The Baptists were prominent in the religious and political movements of the seventeenth century and were pioneers in the struggle for freedom of conscience and religious liberty. The great Baptist John Bunyan is famous for his book *Pilgrim's Progress.*

From the nineteenth century onwards the majority of Baptists have had open communion for all and not just baptized believers and even follow the Bunyan tradition of open membership welcoming 'all who love the Lord Jesus Christ', hence the many Union churches of Baptists and Congregationalists.

There was a zeal for mission among the Baptists from very early days. Action began with William Carey, the shoemaker minister who wrote a book called *Enquiry into the Obligation of Christians to use means for the*

Baptism by total immersion

Conversion of the Heathen in which he insisted that the Bible commanded men to go out and convert the heathen. Under Carey's lead the Baptist Missionary Society was founded and Carey went to India as its first missionary He set up the first Christian university of the East at Serampore near Calcutta and in one generation translated as many versions of the Bible as the whole world had produced in seventeen centuries.

There are 3,600 churches of the Baptist Union of Great Britain and Ireland each of which is responsible for its own life and witness, including the choice of its minister who like the Congregational minister can choose whether he will wear the clerical collar and gown. The churches are gathered in local unions which belong in turn to the Baptist Union, meeting in annual assembly under an elected president. In large areas there are general superintendents who confer with each other regularly.

The Society of Friends (Quakers)

'Quaker' was the nickname given to George Fox (1624-91) in 1650 by a judge whom he told to 'quake and fear at the word of God'. The Quakers themselves use the term to refer to the spiritual tremblings in their meetings. Since early in the nineteenth century the usual title given to Quakers has been The Society of Friends.

The movement was organized in 1668 by Fox who had given up his membership of the Church and had come to rely on the inner light of the living Christ. He began to preach that the truth is to be found in the voice of God speaking directly to man's soul. He soon gathered followers and formed a simple organization. The Quakers were persecuted till the Toleration Act but unlike other Nonconformists they refused to meet in secret.

The Friends represent a type of Reformation Protestantism developed among Christians whose spiritual needs were met neither by the Church of England nor by the Nonconformists. Basing their religion on the belief that God speaks directly to the heart of every man, they reject all ceremony. They have no creed, sacraments, ordained ministry, ordered services or consecrated buildings. They find the final religious authority neither in the Bible nor in the Church but in the inner light by which God speaks and works in the soul of the individual, freeing him from sin, uniting him with Christ and enabling him to do good.

From the eighteenth century they developed the idea of being a peculiar people. They stood out because of the plain way in which they dressed. They used Christian names only and refused titles, calling each other thou instead of you. They have always been strict pacifists and because they refuse military service and will not take oaths they have often come into conflict with authority. They are particularly well known for their devotion to all kinds of social work to which they have made an enormous contribution in spite of their small numbers. Elizabeth Fry was a very famous Quaker who fought a battle for prison reform in the late eighteenth century.

Although the Friends are too austere to have wide popular appeal, they have nevertheless spread over the world, especially in America where in 1682 William Penn founded Pennsylvania on Quaker principles.

The British membership today is around 25,000 with about 500 meeting places. These are simple rooms where Quakers meet in silence waiting for God to move one of them to speak. Organization is simple and democratic. Each area has a monthly meeting open to all members which deals with business and arranges help for those in need. There are also quarterly and yearly meetings to deal with larger concerns. A permanent meeting for sufferings begun during persecution now deals with hardships all over the world. There are no ordained ministers but in addition to administrative staff and full time workers overseas, there are many voluntary elders responsible for meetings and overseers for pastoral care.

The Brethren
The nineteenth century evangelical movement in the Church of England had far reaching effects. It not only stirred the Free Churches but brought into being new groups which emphasized personal devotion to Christ and wanted to revive Puritan moral standards. Among these the Brethren are prominent. This group was founded in Dublin by J.N.Darby, a former Anglican clergyman, in 1827, but two or three years later the centre of the movement was established in Plymouth. This is the reason for the common name Plymouth Brethren.

The Brethren are very puritanical in the way they behave and reject wordly pleasure. There is no organized ministry but they have Sunday meetings for simple prayer services, Bible readings, preaching and include breaking bread as a symbol of unity in Christ and the appointed means to proclaim the Cross. They are conservative in their attitude to and use of the Bible. In spite of their concern for unity they have tended to split into open and exclusive or closed groups. Closed groups have no contact of any kind with people outside their membership even if this means cutting themselves off from members of their own family.

The groups are small but are to be found all over Britain, on the Continent and in the USA. Because they believe that statistics are contrary to the scriptures the Brethren do not state the size of their membership but there are probably upwards of 80,000 in Britain. They engage in missionary work in India, Africa and Latin America.

6 Methodism

Methodism resulted from the great revival of personal religion within the Church of England through the work of two Anglican clergymen John and Charles Wesley and their followers.

Early in the eighteenth century, John Wesley joined a group of students at Oxford in a society for prayer, Bible study, regular communion and charitable work. From the regularity of their strict Christian practice the members of this 'Holy Club' were nicknamed Methodists.

In 1735, some years after ordination, Wesley went on a mission to Georgia, USA. This proved a failure and after a short unhappy stay he returned home in deep spiritual distress. On the outward journey he had met some Moravian Brethren whose deep spiritual life made a profound impression on him. On his return he resumed contact with their kind of piety through the religious societies of the time. From them he learned the need for personal faith and during a society meeting in London in May 1738 he experienced what he knew to be true conversion. This was the beginning of a life long preaching ministry. Remaining an Anglican priest he travelled over the United Kingdom seeking to instil a new vitality into the lethargic religion of the day.

When refused permission to preach in parish churches Wesley said 'I regard the whole world as my parish' and went into the open air enlisting and organizing lay preachers to help in the work of evangelism. In spite of what was often violent opposition the movement stirred and began to change the country. As the number of converts both within and outside the Church grew, so did the need for organization to train them in disciplined Christian living. Societies were formed which deepened spiritual life within the Church but met outside the times of regular Church worship. Wesley had no intention of separating from the Church of England and did not want to appear to be in competition. Unhappily the old bottle proved unable to contain the new wine and separation became inevitable. The critical date is probably 1784.

The Anglican clergy reacted against Methodist enthusiasm. They offered little hospitality to the converts of the movement, most of whom had no previous connection with the established or indeed any Church. When separate places of meeting had to be built the law required them to be registered as dissenting chapels. Matters came to a head in connection with America. Anglican settlers, including Methodists, were under the care of the Bishop of London. The government had resisted all efforts to set up an episcopate for the colonies and after the War of Independence it was not possible to ordain priests in England to serve in the new nation. So it was under a sense of pressure that in 1784 Wesley conducted ordinations himself. Some time earlier he had reached the conclusion that there was no essential difference between bishop and presbyter. So it was as a presbyter bishop in the New Testament sense that he ordained deacons and priests to serve in America. He also appointed an Anglican priest Thomas Coke as superintendent. for Methodists in America. On arrival Coke began to call himself bishop.

However well intentioned, this was a breach of church order and made the separation of the Methodists from the mother church inevitable. In 1784 'the people called Methodists' were recognized by law. Their chapels were held in trust for them and the annual conference of preachers first held in 1744 was regarded as their respresentative body. When Wesley died in 1791 many of the 135,000 members still regarded themselves as Anglicans but loyalty to Methodism was growing. A Plan of Pacification at the 1795 conference allowed services in the chapels to be held at the same time as those in parish churches and Methodist services of Holy Communion could be administered by those whom the conference authorized to do so.

This marks the final separation of Methodism from the Church of England. Since then the Societies have been organized as a Church with regular ordination of ministers on the Presbyterian pattern. In this form Methodism has spread all over the world through missionary work and colonial expansion. Still comparatively small in Great Britain, Methodist members total some eighteen million and there are upwards of forty million adherents.

The Methodist Church accepts the Creeds and the principles of the Protestant Reformation. It welcomes as members all people who sincerely desire to be saved from their sins through faith in Christ and give evidence of this in their conduct and way of life and seek to have fellowship with Christ and his Church by taking up the duties and privileges of Methodism.

Methodism lays special emphasis on the New Testament teaching that all who believe in Christ may have assurance through the witness of the Holy Spirit that they are reconciled with God and that with God's help they may grow in holiness, overcoming sin under the rule of perfect love. There is a strong Puritan element in the Methodist view of personal behaviour as shown by the fact that the majority will not drink alcohol.

Methodist worship is of the free type with hymns, extempore prayer and emphasis on the sermon. In addition to scripture as the sole rule for faith and life and the Creeds, certain standard Methodist doctrines are laid down in Wesley's *Notes on the New Testament* and his *Forty Four Standard Sermons.* All Methodist preachers must read and give general assent to these. They emphasize that Christ died for all men and that God's offer of salvation is open to all. This doctrine of free grace set out in the notes and sermons of John Wesley was most effectively expressed in the hymns of Charles Wesley.

Methodists continue to lay great stress on human fellowship. This does not just mean human friendship, rather it means that all members have an obligation to exercise self control and mutual control as part of the development of Christian life.

In Britain the supreme governing body of the Methodist Church is the annual conference which has an elected president who is always a minister and a lay vice-president. The members are made up of an equal number of ordained and laity elected annually. Methodism has a connectional system whereby the country is divided into thirty-four districts each under a ministerial chairman appointed by conference. The districts, whose representative synods meet twice a year, are divided into circuits of one or many churches with ministerial staff under a superintendent. There are circuit quarterly meetings and local leaders' meetings to direct and supervise worship and work. Ministers, who are often invited by circuits but always appointed by conference, serve for several years under the system which allows for regular change.

Today there are about three quarters of a million members with 4,000 ministers and 12,000 churches. This difference in numbers between ministers and churches underlines the great emphasis laid by Methodism on the cooperation of ministers and laity, including the local preachers who are trained and appointed to conduct worship. In a few cases where there is

John Wesley   **William Booth**

The Slough Salvation Army band

urgent pastoral need a local preacher may be given dispensation to administer Holy Communion.

The Salvation Army

The Salvation Army has certain connections with Methodism as it was founded in 1865 by a Methodist minister, William Booth, in the East End of London. Inspired by the Methodist tradition he absorbed its spirit of evangelism and urge to serve the present age. Finding the organization of the Church at that time too constricting he broke away and in 1878 developed his movement on military lines with himself as general, his ministers as officers and the members as soldiers, all in uniform.

The Army which now operates in 71 countries is ready to meet any emergency and able to perform many Christian services for which the traditional churches are not always equipped. It is divided into territories, provinces, divisions and corps. The last, the local unit, supports its own officers. The general is elected by the High Council and directs the various branches through area and local commanders.

The doctrines are not essentially different from the common body of Protestant belief although they are more evangelical in nature and lay great stress on conversion. The Army does not observe the sacraments but maintains practices which they believe conserve the realities of baptism and Holy Communion. The officers minister to regular congregations which they lead out from the citadel to serve the neighbourhood. The brass band is used in worship and is a well known feature of the Army.

In this country there are well over a thousand Army centres with twice that number of trained and commissioned officers.

7 In faith to unity

It has so often been said the Catholic and Protestant are separated by their different views on the ultimate religious authority. What must I obey to be saved? The Catholic will answer 'the voice of the Church' and the Protestant will answer 'the Bible'.

There is some truth in this rough analysis as Catholic and Protestant have tended to emphasize Church and Bible respectively. But to oversimplify the issue will be misleading. At most we can say that Protestantism has tended to give greater authority to the inner witness based on experience and illuminated by the Holy Spirit than to any external authority.

How do things stand today? What are the main characteristics that British Protestant denominations have in common? Although it has never been easy for Protestants to agree on a positive statement of what they do have in common there are certain fundamental principles of the Protestant Reformation which form a common heritage.

Protestants claim that the Bible is the primary source of revealed truth. Biblical revelation is far more important than the traditions of men. The principle which must govern the life and thought of the Christian and the Church is the word as revealed by Jesus Christ which the Church proclaims and through which it is continually subject to reform. When the word is read, preached and visibly set forth in the sacraments Christ is offered. The Church which is the company of believers who are taught by the Gospel and to whom the sacraments are administered must live by this word.

'When Christ is known we have the sum of the Gospel'. This comment by Calvin explains the central Protestant emphasis on Christ as the one mediator between God and man. It means that everything in religion is bound up with the events of Jesus' earthly life and his sacrifice on the cross. It means that Christ is Lord and Saviour and exists now as a life giving spirit, the Holy Ghost.

From this follows the formula which sums up the central Protestant belief in justification by faith. This was not a new teaching invented in the sixteenth century. It was the revival of the New Testament truth that the sinner can come before God only through personal trust in Jesus Christ. No man can earn salvation by good deeds that a man must do and can do are the result of this but not its cause.

Faith is man's response to the grace of God. God takes the initiative in man's salvation. Man who is a sinner can put his trust in God's mercy only because God has made it possible. This conviction that God's love anticipates man's repentance and leads to forgiveness is at the heart of Protestant Christianity. It means that God's relation to man as revealed in Christ is personal. This assurance revealed at a time when doctrine was expressed in legal and commercial terms and when Christian action involved so much that was merely superficial, has never been surrendered. Generations of believers have learned to build the foundation of a good life on faith in the living God.

The belief that God accepts men for themselves rather than through the power of priests underlies the Reformation emphasis on the priesthood of all believers. Against the view that only the priest had the power to open or bar the way to God, the Reformers maintained the scriptural truth that God in Christ is available to every believer. The immediacy of this contact between God and man does not mean that whatever any man happens to believe or feel is necessarily true. Nor does it mean that each man can believe what he likes regardless of the Bible and the Church. The point is that no earthly authority can claim to come between a man and the truth and compel him to believe something else. Nor again does the doctrine mean that each man is his own priest so that he has no need of the Church. Luther explains:

At the Eucharist we all break bread beside our priest and minister and around him, men and women, young and old, master and servant, mistress and maid, all holy priests together. sanctified by the blood of Christ. We are there in our priestly dignity . . . . we do not let the priest proclaim for himself the ordinance of Christ; but he is the mouth piece of us all and we all say it with him in our hearts and with true faith in the Lamb of God who feeds us with his Body and Blood.

Any suggestions that any man can do anything in the Church is a perversion of the truth of the priesthood of all believers. Within the priestly body there are many tasks to be done and each member has his own calling. But all are required to do their own believing and have the responsibility of witnessing to Christ by what they are, say and do.

Clearly we are here at a deeper level than that of arguing about whether church government should be episcopal or presbyterian and similar topics which have led to such controversy and caused so much separation. The present century has seen many Protestants return to the positive aspects of their Reformation heritage with a growing desire to overcome the old divisions. There is a growing willingness to see that all men in Christ belong together and that each side has much to give and to receive from the other.

Suggestions for further reading

R.J.W. Bevan *The Churches and Christian Unity* OUP 1963
O. Chadwick *The Reformation* Penguin 1964
H. Davies *The English Free Churches* OUP 1963
R.E. Davies *Methodism* Penguin 1963
B.L. Manning *Essays in Orthodox Dissent* Independent Press
2nd Impression 1953
S.C. Neill *Anglicanism* Penguin 1965
A.C. Outler *John Wesley* OUP 1964
E.A. Payne *The Free Church Tradition in the Life of England* Hodder 1965
A.C. Underwood *A History of the English Baptists* Baptist Union 1947
M. Ward *The Churches Move Together* Denholm House Press 1968

Index

Act of Supremacy   21,23
Act of Uniformity   23,26
Anglican Church   7,8,9,21,24,25
   theology   27
Apostles' Creed   9,28
Archbishop of Canterbury   20,21,23,25, 29
Augsburg Confession   19

baptism   9,10,16,28,36
   of Jesus Christ   6
Baptists   9,10,36
   organizations   38
Bible   5,9,15,17,21,22,24,30,35,36,44
   English   22
Bible Society   27
Brethren, the   39
Brown, Robert   35
Bunyan, John   37
burial   12

Calvin, John   15,30
Calvinism   30
Carey, William   37
Catholic Church   15,16,18,19
Catholic Revival   27
Charles I   25,26,36
Christmas   12
Church, the Christian   5,7,10,14,16
Church of England   15,20,24,27,35
   and the State   24
   effect of the Reformation on   24
   expansion   29
   government of   24
   history   20
   organization   28
Church of Scotland   15,33

Civil War   24
confirmation   10
Congregationalism   25,35
Coventry cathedral   8
Cranmer   21,22,23
Cromwell   26,36

dissolution of monasteries   21

Easter Sunday   13
Edward VI   22,23
Elizabeth I   23,24,25
Erasmus   21
Establishment   24,33,35
Evangelical revival   27

Fox, George   38
Fry, Elizabeth   39

God, nature of   5
godparents   9
Good Friday   13

Henry VIII   21,23
holidays   12
Holy Communion   10,16,17,18,22,28
Holy Spirit   5,6,13,36
Holy Trinity   5
Hus, Jan   15

indulgences   16,18
Interdict   16

James I   25,32
James II   27
Jesus Christ   5,6,9,10,12,13,18,44
Jews   6,7

Knox, John   32

Lambeth conferences   20,29
last judgment   12
Lollards   18,21
Luther, Martin   15,16,17,18,21,30,33,
45

marriage   11
Mary   22,23
Messiah   5
Methodism   27,40,43

New Testament   5,7,28
95 Theses   16,18

Old Testament   5,7,28

Penn, William   39
Pontius Pilate   6
Prayer, Book of Common   22,23,25,26,
27,29
Presbyterian Church   15,22,25,26,27,30
organization   36
Protestant Churches   14,17,19
similarities of denominations   44
differences with Roman Catholic   44

Puritans   25,26,27,32

Quakers   38

Reformation   14,20,24,45
Anglican   15,21,25,28,29
challenges to 16th century Church
17
heart of theology   18
Lutheran   15,18,19
resurrection   7,12,13

Salisbury cathedral   8
Salvation Army   43
Smyth, John   32

Ten Commandments   7
Toleration Act   27
39 Articles of Religion   24

Wesley, John   40
Wiclif, John   15,21
Whitsunday   13
worship   9